The Rainbo

A Guide to Married Life for Gay Couples

A comprehensive self-help book designed to inspire, inform, and empower gay couples in their journey of marriage. Packed with practical tips, explorative activities and guidance on building a fulfilling marriage with strong communication and collaboration. Celebrating the uniqueness of LGBTQ+ relationships while providing the tools to nurture growth, resilience and a legacy of love.

Created By
Sky Adams

A @JourneyJunkieBooks Self-Help Series

The Roadmap

In this self-help book, embark on a transformative journey to strengthen and celebrate your love story as a gay couple. Each chapter guides you through essential aspects of a fulfilling marriage, offering valuable insights and practical strategies to build a strong foundation. From embracing your unique love story and fostering communication to navigating family dynamics and nurturing intimacy, this comprehensive guide is tailored to the specific needs of gay couples. Learn to support personal growth, cultivate gratitude and create a lasting legacy of love and inclusivity for a deeply connected and fulfilling marriage.

Chapter 1: Embracing Your Unique Love Story
Celebrate the beautiful diversity of your love story and embrace your individuality as a gay couple. Learn how to honor your shared history while appreciating the unique journey that brought you together.

Chapter 2: Building a Foundation of Communication
Communication is the cornerstone of a strong marriage. Discover effective communication techniques tailored to the specific needs of gay couples, fostering understanding, and deepening your emotional connection.

Chapter 3: Navigating Family and Social Relationships
Navigate the complexities of family and social dynamics as a gay couple. Gain insights and strategies to foster positive relationships with both supportive and challenging individuals in your lives.

Chapter 4: Collaborative Decision-Making and Conflict Resolution
Learn how to make decisions collaboratively and resolve conflicts in a constructive manner. Gain tools to overcome obstacles together, creating a supportive environment for personal growth and relationship development.

Chapter 5: Cultivating Intimacy and Affection
Explore ways to strengthen intimacy and affection in your marriage. From small gestures to nurturing emotional intimacy, discover ways to keep the spark alive in your relationship.

Chapter 6: Fostering Personal Growth Within Your Marriage
Encourage personal growth and self-discovery within the context of your marriage. Support each other's individual journeys while growing together as a couple.

Chapter 7: Cultivating Gratitude and Building a Lasting Legacy
Gratitude can transform your marriage. Learn how to cultivate a sense of appreciation for one another and create a lasting legacy of love, compassion, and inclusivity.

Chapter 1:
Embracing Your Unique Love Story

Welcome to "The Rainbow Journey: A Guide to Married Life for Gay Couples." Buckle up, because we're about to dive into an exhilarating expedition, celebrating the beautiful diversity of love stories within the gay/LGBTQ+ community. This isn't your typical self-help book; it's a roadmap tailored to the fabulous uniqueness of gay marriages!

We're not just another chapter in the book of love; we're the dazzling cover with a story that's authentically ours. Our love stories are kaleidoscopes of colors, each one different, mesmerizing, and uniquely extraordinary. Together, we'll embrace what makes us special as gay individuals navigating married life, tapping into that fierce pride that sets our love apart.

While the journey of love knows no boundaries, our voyage as a gay married couple has its own twists and turns. We've been through challenges, fought for our rights, and rejoiced in victories that shaped our experiences. The historical context of the gay rights movement is etched into our souls, reminding us of the progress we've made and the work that still lies ahead. So, grab your partner's hand, and let's embark on this adventure together.

Throughout these pages, we'll laugh, reflect, and grow. It's not just about the destination—it's about cherishing every step along the way.

Understanding the Historical Context

Let's take a moment to appreciate the journey that brought us here. You know, history is like the epic backdrop to our love story—a vibrant tapestry woven with bravery, resilience, and progress. It's important to know where we came from to fully grasp the significance of our own adventure.

The challenges and triumphs of the gay rights movement paved the way for us to stand here, hand in hand, ready to exchange our vows. We owe so much to those trailblazers who dared to dream of a world where love knows no limits, where hearts could intertwine without judgment, and where LGBTQ+ individuals could be unapologetically themselves. Their courage and determination laid the foundation for the love stories we get to write today.

And can we talk about the moment same-sex marriage became legit? Oh, it was a game-changer! The world suddenly lit up with colors and inclusivity, like a kaleidoscope of love and acceptance. Recognizing this milestone gives power to our love, knowing that our commitment is now officially recognized and celebrated, just like any other love story out there. It's not just a legal victory; it's an affirmation of the love that knows no gender, no race, no boundaries. We're a part of this profound shift, this awakening of love's boundless possibilities. No more hiding in the shadows, no more feeling like our love was somehow less. We were finally free to love boldly and unapologetically, like an explosion of light and joy. Our love story is unique, beautiful, and valid in every way. It's an anthem of authenticity and celebration, and it resonates with countless others in the LGBTQ+ community who have faced similar struggles and triumphs.

So here's to celebrating our history, to cherishing our journey, and to knowing that our love is unstoppable. It's not confined by any rules or boundaries. Love is love, and it's a force that's changing the world, one heart at a time. Cheers to us and the beautiful love we share!

Reflecting on Your Love Story

Alright you gay little lovebirds, get ready for a trip down memory lane! It's time to relive the epic moments in the history of your relationship that brought you both together and made your love story one for the books. So grab your coziest blanket, snuggle up close, and let's dive right in!

It's time to collaborate and pinpoint one answer for each question. Together, you'll celebrate the journey that has shaped your love story and discover the magical moments that make your bond truly extraordinary.

What was that serendipitous moment when your paths first crossed, and you knew there was something special between you?

_____

_____

_____

_____

Think back to your favorite shared memory before getting married. What made that moment so unforgettable and full of joy?

_____

_____

_____

How have you both overcome hurdles together, supporting each other through tough times and becoming even stronger as a team?

_____

_____

_____

_____

_____

What's the most unexpected adventure or experience that brought you even closer as a couple?

_____

_____

_____

_____

_____

Now, let's relive that "aha" moment when you both realized you wanted to spend the rest of your lives together. What made it crystal clear that you were meant to be?

_____

_____

_____

Embracing Individuality

Embracing individuality in a gay marriage is a total game-changer, trust me! It's like having this awesome power couple dynamic where both partners can be their fabulous, authentic selves. You know, in a world that sometimes wants us to fit into these little boxes, embracing who we are as individuals is a rebellion of self-love and empowerment. When you and your partner can be your true selves without judgment, it creates this incredible bond of trust and understanding.

Imagine cheering each other on as you both pursue your passions and dreams, knowing that you've got each other's backs no matter what. It's about saying, "Hey, I love you for who you are, quirks and all!" Embracing individuality in your gay marriage allows you both to grow together and as individuals, becoming stronger and more fulfilled in the process.

And you know what's the best part? It's like a daily dose of excitement and discovery! You get to learn more about each other every day, appreciating those little things that make you both unique and extraordinary.

What are 3 characteristic each of you bring to the table that brings balance to your relationship?

Partner 1:

1. _____

2. _____

3. _____

Partner 2:

1. _____

2. _____

3. _____

Embracing Your LGBTQ+ Identity

Let's talk about why being confidently and unashamedly gay in your marriage is incredibly important. When you both stand tall and proud in your LGBTQ+ identity, it's like this magnetic force that draws you closer together, celebrating who you are as individuals and as a united front.

Being confident and unashamed of being gay within your marriage creates this safe space where you can be your authentic selves. It's like the ultimate love letter to each other, saying, "I love you for exactly who you are, and I'm proud to be by your side." It nurtures a deep sense of trust and vulnerability, allowing you to share your fears, joys, and dreams without hesitation.

And let me tell you, when you're confidently embracing your LGBTQ+ identity, it's contagious! It's like this ripple effect of love and acceptance that extends beyond your marriage. By proudly showing the world your love, you become trailblazers, paving the way for others to embrace their true selves without shame.

So, let your love shine brightly with confidence and pride! It's not just important; it's a powerful declaration of your love's authenticity. Embrace your LGBTQ+ identity, be unapologetically gay, and watch your marriage become a beacon of love and inspiration for all. You're changing the world, one fabulous moment at a time!

Embracing the Journey

You did it! Congrats on conquering the first leg of "The Rainbow Journey." Now, prepare yourselves for the exciting adventures ahead! Embrace that one-of-a-kind love story you've got, and let it be your guiding star as we move forward together.

Be proud, be unapologetically you, 'cause trust me, your love is nothing short of extraordinary. In the upcoming chapters, we'll dive deeper into the magic of communication, the secrets of intimacy, and how to create a legacy of love that'll blow your minds.

So, stay pumped, keep that adventurous spirit alive, and keep your hearts wide open to the love that's waiting for you. Get ready, my fellow explorers, 'cause we're about to experience the best moments of this incredible journey!

Notes & takeaways from this chapter:

_____

_____

_____

_____

_____

_____

_____

_____

_____

_____

_____

_____

_____

_____

Chapter 2:
Building a Foundation of Communication

Embracing Open and Honest Dialogue

Let's dive into the heart of communication, where the magic happens. In a gay marriage, creating a safe space for open and honest dialogue is everything. It's like this secret sauce that keeps the love flowing and the connection strong. So how do we do it?

First off, active listening is the name of the game. When your partner speaks, tune in with your heart and ears wide open. It's about understanding their thoughts and feelings without interrupting or jumping to conclusions. And when it's your turn to share, go for it with vulnerability and authenticity. Let those thoughts and emotions flow like a rainbow river!

Now, we know that tough conversations might come up now and then. But guess what? You got this! Approach those moments with empathy and understanding, even if you don't see eye to eye. It's all about respecting each other's perspectives and finding that middle ground where compromise blooms. Embrace the power of communication, and you'll see your emotional connection soar to new heights!

How can we rock active listening in our marriage? Share three simple ways to better understand and support each other's thoughts and feelings.

1. _____

2. _____

3. _____

When it comes to tricky topics, how can we create a safe and chill space for open talks? Give two ideas to ensure we both feel heard and respected during these conversations.

1. _____

2. _____

Nurturing Emotional Intimacy

let's talk emotional intimacy—the secret ingredient to keep that spark alive in your gay marriage. It's like this beautiful dance where you both connect on a soul-deep level. So, how do we nurture it and let it blossom?

Take some time to share your hopes, dreams, and fears with each other. Open up those emotional treasure chests and let your partner in. It's like this magical exchange of trust and vulnerability that strengthens your bond. And remember, it's okay to support and validate each other's emotions. That's like sprinkling fairy dust of love and understanding all around!

Celebrate your similarities and differences! Embrace the unique blend that makes you both the fabulous couple you are. And yes, disagreements might happen along the way, but that's okay. Embrace those moments with respect and curiosity. It's like this beautiful journey of growth and learning together. Oh, and don't forget to throw in some laughter and light-heartedness. It's like the cherry on top that adds that extra sparkle to your emotional intimacy dance!

Celebrating Similarities and Differences

It's time to celebrate the magic of you both—the similarities and the differences that make your love story one-of-a-kind. In a gay marriage, it's like a fusion of energies, creating this dazzling connection. So let's bask in the glory of your unique blend!

Embrace those similarities, like the shared interests, passions, and values that brought you together. It's like a cosmic alignment that says, "Hey, we're meant to be!" But don't forget to celebrate the differences too! It's like this colorful palette that adds depth and dimension to your love story.

Now, we know that differing viewpoints might arise, and that's totally normal. So let's navigate those moments with grace and respect. It's like this treasure hunt, where you discover new facets of each other's personalities. Embrace the diversity within your union, and let your love shine brighter than a supernova! Both partners bring their own unique skillsets and characteristics to their marriage forming the perfect balance.

What shared interests, passions, or values brought us together, and how do they strengthen our bond?

_____

_____

_____

How do we celebrate and embrace our differences, navigating differing viewpoints with grace and respect to keep our love shining brightly?

_____

_____

_____

Resolving Conflict Constructively

Alright, you gay dynamic duo, let's talk about conflict, because guess what? It's not the end of the world. In a gay marriage, conflict can be a catalyst for growth and understanding. So how do we handle it constructively?

First things first, let's arm ourselves with some seriously effective conflict resolution techniques. When those stormy moments hit, and the heat is on, take a deep breath and remember, you're not opponents; you're a team, an unbeatable duo. So, together, let's find that sweet spot—the middle ground— where both of you feel heard, valued, and respected. Let's say no to those destructive communication traps that we all know too well, like those painful "you always" and "you never" statements. Instead, let's focus on building bridges, not walls, and create a safe space for open dialogue.

Now, here's a secret weapon that can turn conflict on its head—forgiveness! It's like this magical elixir that can heal wounds and mend hearts. We're all human, and let's face it, we make mistakes. But here's the deal, embracing forgiveness with open arms is not a weakness; it's a superpower! So, let's practice the art of forgiving each other and ourselves, and watch our love bloom like a lush garden after a refreshing rain.

So, you got this, love champs! Let's navigate conflict like the pros we are, knowing that every challenge we conquer together is a stepping stone to a stronger bond. It's like this empowering dance of resilience and growth, where we learn more about each other and ourselves. So let's strap on our resilience boots and dance through the rain, bringing us even closer while the sun peeks through forming that pretty little rainbow you're building together.

How do you handle conflicts constructively as a gay married couple, ensuring that both of you feel heard and respected?

Instead of resorting to negative "you always," and "You never" statements, what are some ways we can shift the dialogue?

How do you practice forgiveness in your relationship, and how does it contribute to strengthening your bond as a couple?

_____

_____

Notes & takeaways from this chapter:

_____

_____

_____

_____

_____

_____

_____

_____

_____

_____

Chapter 3:
Navigating Family and Social Relationships

The Allies in Your Corner

When you've got an awesome crew of people in your life who wholeheartedly embrace your love story, no matter who you love, it's like having your own personal cheerleaders, hyping you up in every adventure and challenge. Their acceptance creates this amazing sense of belonging and support that just makes your marriage feel secure, makes it feel "normal." You feel like you can be your true selves without any worries or judgment, and it's the most freeing feeling ever!

Having a solid squad of family and friends who totally embrace your gay marriage is like having this treasure chest of love and wisdom right there with you. When these amazing peeps stand by your side, it creates this chill and supportive space where you can learn and grow together. They bring in their unique experiences and insights, and you do the same, making it a cool exchange of knowledge and understanding. Their acceptance creates this awesome vibe of openness and learning, where you can freely share your thoughts and feelings, and they feel comfortable doing the same. It's like this two-way street of growth and understanding, where you learn from them, and they learn from you, and it builds this rad tapestry of love and learning that bonds you even closer.

So here's to embracing those who embrace us, to celebrating love in all its colors, and to creating a world where everyone can feel this incredible sense of belonging and acceptance.

How does the acceptance and support from our family and friends impact our marriage?

_____

_____

_____

In what specific ways have our family and friends contributed to our growth as a couple, and how has their acceptance created an open and supportive environment for sharing thoughts and feelings?

_____

_____

_____

YES   NO   **Do you feel supported in your family?**

YES   NO   **Do you feel supported in your friend circle?**

YES   NO   **Do you feel supported at work?**

List your top 5 supportive family members or friends:

1. _____

2. _____

3. _____

4. _____

5. _____

Navigating Challenging Relationships

Now, let's talk about those family members or friends who might still be wrapping their heads around the LGBTQ+ world. Navigating your gay marriage when there are not-so-accepting family members can be a tough challenge, but fear not, fellow love warriors, I've got some strategies to help you through it!

First off, remember that your love story is beautiful and valid, and no one else's opinion can change that. Stay true to yourselves and don't let anyone dim your rainbow light.

When facing unsupportive family members, it's important to set healthy boundaries. You and your partner are a team, and protecting your relationship from negativity is crucial. Have an open and honest conversation with each other about how you want to handle these situations together. Maybe it means limiting interactions with the not-so-accepting folks or having a plan for dealing with potential conflicts. Keep the communication lines open between you two, so you can face these challenges united.

Building a strong support network outside of your immediate family can also be a game-changer. Seek out LGBTQ+ inclusive communities and friends who celebrate and uplift your love. Having a group of people who get you and stand by your side can provide a safe and nurturing space to share experiences and seek advice. Remember, love is love, and surrounding yourselves with people who believe in your love story can make all the difference in the world. Keep shining bright, my friends, and know that you are never alone on this beautiful journey.

What are some healthy boundaries we can set to protect our relationship when dealing with unsupportive family, friends or peers?

_____

_____

_____

How can we communicate with compassion and understanding to address the concerns of unsupportive individuals?

_____

_____

_____

What strategies can we use to navigate potential conflicts and maintain our emotional well-being in the face of negativity?

_____

_____

_____

Do you have unsupportive people in your life? List any below:

1. _____

2. _____

3. _____

4. _____

5. _____

Building a Supportive Network

In this section, we're all about building a dream team of friends and allies who embrace and celebrate your love! Having a supportive network is like having a cozy blanket on a chilly day—it wraps you in warmth and love. These are the people who see you, support you, and uplift you for exactly who you are.

Building this network starts with finding inclusive spaces and resources that connect you with like-minded individuals. It might be an LGBTQ+

community center, a social group, or even online platforms where you can share experiences and connect with others. These spaces can become your tribe, your chosen family, who'll celebrate your love with open arms.

Creating a safe and supportive environment for each other within your social circles is equally important. Surround yourselves with friends who love you both for the beautiful beings you are. As a gay couple, having friends who appreciate your relationship as an integral part of your lives will bring joy and fulfillment to your journey together. These connections will become the pillars of your support system, encouraging you to soar higher and love even stronger.

Do you feel like you have a support network of like-minded individuals?

_____

_____

_____

Who is the number 1 fan of your marriage?

_____

List 4 ways you can possibly build your network of support:

1. _____

2. _____

3. _____

4. _____

Boundaries and Self-Care

Let's talk about boundaries, the superhero capes that protect our relationship and emotional well-being. In a world where there are different opinions and expectations, setting healthy boundaries is crucial. Establishing what is acceptable and what isn't within your relationship will create a safe and loving space for both of you.

Practicing self-care techniques is essential to nurture your individual selves and maintain a strong foundation for your marriage. As a couple, you might have different ways of recharging and finding inner peace. Embrace those differences and support each other's well-being, knowing that taking care of yourselves allows you to be the best partners for one another.

Lastly, remember to be kind to yourselves and embrace your fabulous identities with pride. Your love story is extraordinary, and every part of it—the joys, the challenges, and the uniqueness—makes it something truly special. Be proud of the love you share and the resilience you embody as a gay couple navigating the beautiful complexities of life and love.

By delving into the intricacies of navigating family and social relationships, you and your partner will emerge with a treasure trove of insights and strategies. Together, you'll cultivate a harmonious and supportive network around your marriage. Let's celebrate the beautiful diversity of your love story while appreciating the unique journey that brought you together as a resilient and united couple.

What are some ways you recharge and find inner peace as a couple?

_____

_____

_____

What are some ways you individually practice self-care?

Partner 1:

_____

_____

_____

_____

Partner 2:

_____

_____

_____

_____

Notes & takeaways from this chapter:

Chapter 4:
Collaborative Decision-Making and Conflict Resolution

The Power of Teamwork in Decision-Making

Oh, the awesome magic of teamwork in a gay marriage! You two are like a dynamic duo with superpowers, ready to take on the world together. But guess what? It gets even cooler! Learning to communicate openly and honestly about your needs and preferences is like having a secret language that unlocks a deeper understanding of each other's dreams and aspirations. You're not just partners; you're a dream team, and together, you can co-create a future filled with endless possibilities!

Let's face it, being in a gay marriage comes with its own unique challenges, but fear not, because you've got this! Embracing your differences and strengths, and learning to work as a team, is the key to making decisions that feel balanced and supportive for both of you. It's all about recognizing each other's awesomeness and divvying up tasks in a way that feels natural. Decision-making becomes a joyous adventure, knowing that your voices are equally important and heard, valid and supported within your relationship. With this in mind, you have a key to unlocking a stronger bond.

In this magical realm of teamwork, navigating your journey with confidence and love, being open and honest about your needs creates a safe space where both of you can flourish as individuals and as a united couple. It's like having your very own love navigation system, guiding you through life's ups and downs together. From planning your next big adventure to handling the daily stuff, you know you can rely on each other to make decisions as a dynamic duo. So, my fabulous lovebirds, remember that you're not just walking this path together; you're creating it, hand in hand, and that's a bond that's truly extraordinary!

How can we harness the power of teamwork in our marriage to make decisions that feel balanced and supportive for both of us?

_____

_____

_____

Conflict Resolution: Challenges into Opportunities

Alright, let's dive into the nitty-gritty of conflicts because, hey, they happen in every relationship. But no worries, you've totally got this! In a gay marriage, conflict resolution is like flexing a superhero muscle. It's all about tackling those tough moments with empathy and understanding, even when things get a tad heated. Picture it like this: creating a safe space for open communication during conflicts is like sprinkling some magic fairy dust on the situation. You both get to express your emotions freely without any fear of judgment, and that's pretty darn special.

So, get ready to put those active listening skills to the test and validate each other's emotions and perspectives. Believe me, these powerful tools can work wonders, turning disagreements into golden opportunities for growth and connection. Conflict resolution is like this superpower that strengthens your bond as a couple. It's all about navigating those stormy waters together, knowing that you're a united team, facing the world hand in hand.

Remember, love warriors, conflicts are a normal part of any relationship, you have the unique strength to embrace them with empathy and create an even deeper connection with your partner.

Research has shown that conflicts, when managed effectively, can lead to increased understanding, better communication, and greater relationship satisfaction in the long term. Couples who learn to navigate and resolve conflicts together tend to have stronger bonds and a more fulfilling marriage.

Activity: Conflict Management

Find a quiet and comfortable space to talk openly. Take turns sharing your thoughts and feelings about 2 recent conflicts. Think of specific conflicts that caused a significant argument within your relationship.

Now, taking turns, take 3 minutes each to explain your reasoning for why the conflict occurred. Practice active listening and try to understand each other's perspectives.

After you have both had a chance to speak. Take 2 minutes in silence to reflect on how these challenges made you feel, and how they can lead to growth and bring you closer together. What did you learn?

Embrace conflicts as natural parts of any relationship, and approach them with empathy and understanding. By working together, you'll strengthen your bond and grow as a couple. Remember, conflicts can be opportunities for deeper connection in your marriage.

What were some takeaways from this conversation?

_____

_____

_____

_____

_____

_____

_____

_____

_____

_____

Overcoming Obstacles Together

Life's journey may throw some curveballs, but fear not, because you've got your partner right there beside you, ready to take on the world as a united front. In a gay marriage, facing external pressures and societal expectations together strengthens your bond and makes it unbreakable. From supporting each other through tough times to celebrating victories, you've built a fortress of love and understanding that stands tall amidst the challenges you encounter. But guess what? You can level up your relationship game even more!

By developing strategies to manage stress and challenges from external sources, you add an extra layer of armor to protect your love. The outside world may not always understand your unique journey, but together, you can navigate it with grace and resilience. Embracing your identity and love story with pride will shield you from negativity and allow you to stay true to yourselves. Remember, you're true love warriors, and when you face obstacles together, nothing can bring you down.

Take a moment to bask in your resilience as a couple, appreciating the strength that comes from overcoming challenges. Every hurdle you conquer becomes a stepping stone for personal and relationship growth. The experiences you go through together shape and mold your love, making it even more profound and resilient. In the face of adversity, remember that you have each other's backs and hearts, and that powerful connection will see you through it all.

So, my fabulous love duo, embrace the unique challenges that come with being in a gay marriage, and face them together with courage and love. By supporting each other through the ups and downs, you create an unshakable foundation for your relationship. Keep that positive energy flowing and tackle whatever comes your way hand in hand. Your love is a force to be reckoned with, and together, you'll conquer it all with unwavering strength and an abundance of joy. Trust in your love, and know that you have the power to shape your destiny together. Let the world witness the magic of your love story, as you create a future filled with endless possibilities, celebrating your uniqueness every step of the way.

How have external pressures and societal expectations impacted our relationship as a gay couple, and how do we navigate them together as a united front?

_____

_____

_____

What are some strategies we can develop to manage stress and challenges from external sources, and how can we support each other in staying true to our identity and love story?

_____

_____

_____

_____

Reflecting on our journey as a couple, how have we grown stronger and more resilient by facing challenges together, and what are some ways we can continue to strengthen our bond in the face of adversity?

_____

_____

_____

_____

_____

_____

Notes & takeaways from this chapter:

_____

_____

_____

_____

_____

Chapter 5:
Cultivating Intimacy and Affection

Embracing Your Unique Love Languages

Alright, lovebirds, let's talk about the magical realm of love languages! You see, just like a secret code that unlocks the door to your partner's heart, love languages are these awesome ways we show and receive love. As a gay married couple, embracing each other's unique love languages can be a game-changer in keeping that spark alive.

First off, let's decode what these love languages are all about. Dr. Gary Chapman, the love guru, identified five love languages: Words of Affirmation, Acts of Service, Receiving Gifts, Quality Time, and Physical Touch. Each of us has a primary love language that speaks to our heart the loudest. Understanding your partner's love language and vice versa can lead to the most heartwarming and fulfilling expressions of love.

Now, you might wonder, how do I discover my partner's love language and unveil the key to their heart? Fear not, love detective! It's all about observation and communication. Pay close attention to what makes them light up and feel cherished. Do they love hearing sweet words? Are they over the moon when you do something thoughtful for them? Maybe they value quality time or thrive on physical touch. Openly discussing your love languages with your partner can also bring you both closer together, like two love-detective buddies on an exciting mission!

But here's where the magic really happens. As a gay married couple, you have the opportunity to navigate unique challenges and strengthen your connection through love languages. Embracing each other's love languages fosters a deeper understanding of your partner's needs and desires. And guess what? This superpower of love languages can transform the way you express love, making it even more meaningful and heartfelt. So, get ready to sprinkle some love language magic into your marriage and watch your love story blossom like never before!

Activity: Discover Your Love Languages

Spend a special evening with your partner to discover your love languages. Take a free Love Language Quiz online (just search google!) and share your results. Discuss what each love language means to you and plan an activity that aligns with your partner's love language. Whether it's writing love notes, pampering each other, exchanging thoughtful gifts, having a cozy date night, or enjoying physical touch, embrace each other's unique ways of feeling loved. Reflect on the experience and find ways to incorporate each other's love languages into your daily lives. Enjoy the journey of understanding and cherishing each other even more deeply!

What are each of your love languages? What were some takeaways from this discovery?

_____

_____

_____

_____

_____

_____

_____

Nurturing Emotional Intimacy in a Diverse World

Emotional intimacy, oh, the heart and soul of any relationship! For us gay couples, navigating this captivating territory can bring both delightful rewards and unique challenges. In a world that might not always fully embrace our love, expressing our emotions freely can sometimes feel like dancing through a labyrinth. But worry not, my fellow love warriors! The key to fostering emotional intimacy lies in embracing vulnerability and open communication with your partner. Picture it like this: you both hold hands and leap into the emotional unknown, creating a safe space where feelings flow freely without judgment or hesitation. By baring your hearts to each other, you weave a tapestry of trust and understanding, making your bond unbreakable.

You know, life can throw us some curveballs, especially when we navigate a sometimes less inclusive society. We might encounter external judgments and unwarranted opinions, but fear not! Your love is a force of resilience, and together, you can weather any storm that comes your way. By supporting each other wholeheartedly and maintaining open lines of communication, you forge an unshakable fortress around your relationship. Your love is a sanctuary, a place where you can both find solace and strength in each other's embrace.

So, let's build a haven within your relationship—a nurturing environment where you both uplift and prioritize each other's emotional well-being. Be each other's rock, guiding and supporting each other through life's ups and downs. Celebrate the moments of joy and hold each other close during challenges. In this cocoon of love and care, your emotional intimacy will flourish, and your hearts will dance in harmony, knowing you've found a sanctuary where love always prevails. Together, you'll continue to navigate the enchanting journey of emotional intimacy, growing even closer with each passing day.

Remember, love warriors, emotional intimacy is like a beautiful dance between your hearts, and it thrives when you embrace vulnerability and authentic communication. Your unique challenges and triumphs as a gay couple will only deepen the emotional connection you share. So, take each other's hands, ready to step onto the dance floor of emotional intimacy, and let your hearts sway to the rhythm of love. The world may throw its challenges your way, but with each other's unwavering support, you'll navigate them like the graceful dancers you are, celebrating the love that makes your hearts sing.

Reigniting Your Passion and Romance

Remember, my fabulous lovebirds, keeping the passion alive involves a touch of adventure and a sprinkle of excitement! Explore your relationship through fresh and thrilling experiences that reflect your journey as a couple. Dive into new hobbies together or embark on daring escapades that ignite the spark of joy and curiosity in both of you. Let your imaginations run wild as you surprise each other with playful gestures and heartfelt tokens of your affection. With each playful surprise, you'll remind your partner of the enchanting magic that resides in your love.

Date nights are like precious gems in the crown of a gay married couple's journey. As a gay couple, embracing date nights becomes even more vital because they offer a precious opportunity to celebrate your love. It's a chance to escape into a space where you can be your authentic selves without any reservations and deepen your bond. Each date night becomes a chapter in your love story, filled with laughter, affection, and the magic of being with someone who loves and cherishes you for who you are. So, my fabulous lovebirds, don't underestimate the power of date nights! Embrace them as a source of rejuvenation, and let them remind you of the beauty and strength that lies in your love. Let date nights be your secret formula for resilience, as they hold the power to revitalize your bond and keep the flames of passion dancing. In the journey of a gay marriage, these intimate moments offer a chance to carve out space for love, compassion, and growth. So, step into the magic of date nights and cherish each one as a celebration of your extraordinary love story.

Remember, the key to a successful date night is to focus on each other, enjoy each other's company, and cherish the love you share. Whether you're going on an adventure or having a cozy night in, date nights are an opportunity to nurture your connection and create lasting memories together. Happy dating, lovebirds!

Date Night Ideas

- **Pride Adventure:** Attend a local pride parade or LGBTQ+ event together. Embrace the vibrant atmosphere, celebrate your identity, and show your support for the community.

- **Gay Movie Night:** Have a cozy movie night at home with a selection of LGBTQ+ films. Laugh, cry, and celebrate diverse love stories that resonate with your hearts.

- **Cooking Together:** Try out a new recipe together and have a blast cooking a delicious meal. The kitchen can be a space for shared creativity and a chance to indulge in each other's culinary skills.

- **Outdoor Picnic:** Pack a picnic basket with your favorite snacks and head to a beautiful park or beach. Enjoy each other's company while surrounded by nature's beauty.

- **Game Night Extravaganza:** Have a game night filled with board games, card games, or video games. Engage in friendly competition and create lasting memories. Maybe even spice things up with strip poker!

- **Dance Party in Your Living Room:** Clear the furniture and create a dance floor in your living room. Dance to your favorite tunes and let loose in each other's arms. Slow dance to your first dance wedding song.

- **Stargazing Date:** Find a spot away from city lights, lay down a blanket, and stargaze together. Enjoy the magic of the night sky and the moments of intimacy it brings.

- **Explore a New City:** Plan a day trip to a nearby city or town you both haven't explored. Discover new places, visit local attractions, and indulge in delicious cuisine.

- **Art and Creativity:** Take an art class together or visit a museum or gallery. Embrace your creativity and share in the joy of artistic expression.

- **Spa Night at Home:** Create a spa-like atmosphere at home with scented candles, soothing music, and pampering treatments. Relax and unwind together in a peaceful setting. Spice it up for a happy ending!

- **Beach and a Blanket:** There's nothing quite as romantic as the sound of the ocean waves crashing while you and your love are hand in hand watching the sunset! Go to the beach and have an intimate moment.

- **The Typical Dinner and a Show:** You can't go wrong with the typical date night of spoiling yourselves with a nice dinner. Take this opportunity to try someplace new! Then, go see the latest blockbuster movie, or see if there is a live community theatre production in your hometown and go support the arts. Bonus, you might meet some gay friends at the theatre!

Fostering Intimacy in Physical Affection

Physical affection is a fundamental and cherished aspect of any romantic relationship, and for gay married couples, embracing this form of intimacy takes on a unique significance. According to studies, physical touch is a powerful way to express love and affection, and it plays a vital role in fostering emotional connection and overall relationship satisfaction. However, research also shows that same-sex couples often face unique challenges when it comes to expressing physical affection openly due to societal norms and stigmas. Despite these challenges, LGBTQ+ couples have demonstrated remarkable resilience in navigating external pressures and embracing their physical connection unapologetically.

Understanding the significance of physical affection in a gay marriage is crucial for building a strong and fulfilling partnership. Studies have found that LGBTQ+ individuals tend to value physical touch highly in their relationships, emphasizing the importance of touch as a means of communication and emotional expression. For gay married couples, embracing physical affection can serve as a powerful tool for reinforcing their bond and deepening their emotional connection.

Establishing a safe and nurturing space for physical affection involves open communication and mutual respect. According to a survey conducted by the Family Process Journal, communication about boundaries and desires is especially important for LGBTQ+ couples to ensure both partners feel comfortable and secure in expressing physical intimacy. By actively engaging in conversations about comfort levels, preferences, and consent, gay married couples create an environment of trust and understanding, allowing their physical connection to flourish.

By nurturing intimacy in physical affection, couples can experience heightened relationship satisfaction and emotional well-being. According to the Journal of Homosexuality, same-sex couples who reported higher levels of physical affection and emotional intimacy experienced greater relationship quality and overall life satisfaction. Embracing physical touch, whether it's holding hands, cuddling, or sharing a gentle kiss, allows partners to express their love in a language that speaks directly to the heart.

As a gay married couple, embracing physical affection becomes an empowering act of love and defiance against societal norms. By celebrating and cherishing these intimate moments, LGBTQ+ couples pave the way for greater acceptance and understanding. Through physical connection, they affirm the beauty and strength of their love, creating a positive and affirming narrative for future generations of gay individuals.

In conclusion, physical affection is a precious and vital component of a thriving gay marriage. By acknowledging the unique challenges and joys of physical intimacy, couples can create a safe space where their love can flourish freely. Embracing physical touch as a powerful means of communication and emotional expression strengthens their emotional bond, elevates their relationship satisfaction, and serves as a testament to the resilience and beauty of their love story. Through physical affection, us gay couples embody the strength and authenticity of our love, inspiring a world where all love is celebrated and embraced without reservation.

How has physical intimacy contributed to strengthening your emotional connection as a gay married couple? Have you faced any unique challenges or joys in expressing physical affection openly in society?

_____

_____

_____

_____

_____

What are some ways you are physically affectionate with each other?

_____

_____

_____

How often are you physically affectionate with each other? Do you wish it was more or less?

_____

_____

_____

_____

Notes & takeaways from this chapter:

_____

_____

_____

_____

_____

_____

_____

_____

_____

_____

_____

_____

_____

_____

_____

_____

Chapter 6:
Fostering Personal Growth within Your Marriage

Embracing Individual Journeys

Ah, the beauty of personal growth within a marriage! As a gay couple, you both have unique dreams and aspirations that contribute to your individuality and strengthen the bond you share. Embracing these personal journeys is a powerful way to grow as individuals and as a couple. Openly discussing your goals and passions with each other creates a safe and supportive space to share your dreams. Remember, love warriors, you're in this together, and supporting each other's growth is like adding fuel to the fire of your love.

As you embrace individual journeys, you'll find that your partner's dreams enrich your own. By taking an active interest in each other's pursuits, you become each other's biggest cheerleaders. Celebrate the small milestones and big achievements together, marking them as cherished moments of your shared journey. The freedom to be your authentic selves within the marriage fosters an environment of trust and understanding, where you both feel valued and loved for who you truly are. Embracing your individual passions, achievements and growth allows you to be the best version of yourself for your partner.

How do you support each other's dreams and goals within your marriage, and how has it strengthened your relationship?

_____

_____

_____

What does it mean to create a safe space for open discussions about your passions and aspirations? How has embracing each other's individual journeys enriched your bond as a couple?

_____

_____

_____

Nurturing Self-Discovery

Embracing your authentic selves is the key to unlocking the hidden treasures of a thriving and deeply fulfilling relationship. Take the time to explore the unique identities, interests, and values that make you both extraordinary individuals. As you deepen your understanding of yourselves, you'll discover the incredible power you hold to bring your best selves to the table as loving partners. Encourage each other to embark on this exhilarating journey, knowing that a more self-aware and fulfilled partner can infuse your marriage with even more love and unwavering support.

Being a gay couple means you've faced unique challenges and experiences that have shaped your paths and brought you together. Embracing self-discovery goes hand in hand with embracing your vulnerabilities. Create a safe and trusting space where you can openly share your fears, insecurities, and moments of triumph. It's in these moments of raw vulnerability that the emotional intimacy between you will ignite, forging an unbreakable and profound connection that sets your love apart.

And here's an exciting dose of motivation: Studies have shown that couples who wholeheartedly support each other's personal growth and self-discovery experience unparalleled relationship satisfaction and a love that stands the test of time. So, dive headfirst into this thrilling journey together! Explore your passions, embrace your unique quirks, and celebrate each other's one-of-a-kind magic. This journey of self-discovery will not only deepen your bond but also create a love that's as authentic and powerful as it gets.

Cultivating Shared Growth

As lovebirds navigating this journey together, shared growth is essential. While honoring your individual dreams, find common goals that align with the heart of your relationship. Engage in activities and experiences that bring you both joy and strengthen your bond. It could be anything from traveling to new places, learning new skills together, or even volunteering for a cause you both care about. By cultivating shared growth, you create a powerful sense of unity and a treasure trove of cherished memories that will weave the fabric of your love story.

Shared growth also involves aligning your values and beliefs. Explore your spiritual and philosophical inclinations together, finding common ground that nourishes your love and connection. By sharing in these meaningful aspects of life, you reinforce your shared values and build a strong foundation for the future. Embrace the beauty of growing together and marvel at the richness it brings to your love story.

What activities or experiences bring you both joy and strengthen your bond as a married couple?

_____

_____

_____

Share a memorable moment of shared growth or learning that has enriched your love story as a gay married couple:

_____

_____

_____

_____

_____

Supporting Each Other's Passions

Cheers to being each other's biggest fans! Supporting each other's passions is like giving wings to your partner's dreams. Be each other's cheerleaders, offering encouragement and enthusiasm for the pursuits that set your hearts on fire. Striking a balance between individual passions and the needs of the marriage is a dance worth perfecting. Communicate openly about your desires and create a sense of partnership in supporting one another. Remember, love warriors, when you lift each other up, your love reaches new heights of strength and fulfillment.

Encouraging your partner's passions also means being actively involved in their endeavors. Attend each other's events, performances, or activities, showing your genuine interest and support. Be a source of inspiration and motivation, nurturing the spark of passion within your partner's heart. By fostering an environment where you both feel valued and encouraged, you create a marriage that empowers each other to pursue greatness and fulfillment.

How do you support each others passions?

_____

_____

_____

_____

_____

Overcoming Challenges Together

In the dance of personal growth, challenges may arise, but together you can face them with courage and resilience. Communication is your superpower, so openly discuss any obstacles that come your way. By navigating challenges as a united front, you reinforce the foundation of your marriage and discover newfound strengths within yourselves. Remember, love warriors, the challenges you conquer together become stepping stones that lead to even greater growth and a love that shines brighter with each passing day.

Overcoming challenges also involves embracing change and adaptability. As you both grow and evolve, your marriage may experience shifts that require open-mindedness and understanding. Embrace change as an opportunity for growth and learning, and approach it with a spirit of partnership. By facing challenges together, you fortify your bond and create a sense of security and stability that can weather any storm.

What are 5 of the biggest challenges you've faced as a couple?

1. _____

2. _____

3. _____

4. _____

5. _____

Emotional Intimacy through Personal Growth

Emotional intimacy is the heartbeat of your marriage, and personal growth can amplify its rhythm. As you both embark on individual journeys of self-discovery and development, you create a rich tapestry of emotional connection between you. Communicate openly about your experiences, fears, and joys, deepening your emotional bond. Understanding and supporting each other's growth fosters a sense of safety and vulnerability, allowing love to bloom more profoundly than ever before.

Nurturing emotional intimacy also involves actively listening to each other's stories and experiences. Practice empathy and compassion, acknowledging the significance of your partner's growth moments. By being emotionally available and responsive, you create a space where both of you can express your emotions freely, knowing that you are cherished and valued. Emotional intimacy is a beautiful dance of trust and vulnerability, where you both find solace and strength in each other's love.

Nurturing Love and Connection

Nurturing your love and connection is like tending to a beautiful garden; it requires time, attention, and care. Amidst individual pursuits, make sure to prioritize your relationship. Allocate quality time to cherish each other and engage in activities that reinforce your emotional bond. By nourishing your love, you create a solid foundation for personal growth to thrive, and the roots of your relationship run even deeper. Nurturing your love and connection also involves being attuned to each other's love languages. Remember our exercise from earlier? Understanding how you both prefer to give and receive love is a powerful tool to express your connection in ways that resonate with each other. Whether it's through words of affirmation, acts of service, physical touch, quality time, or gifts, nurturing your love languages deepens your emotional connection and fosters a sense of emotional security within the marriage.

Share one activity or gesture you can incorporate into your routine to nourish your love and create a solid foundation for personal growth within your marriage:

_____

_____

_____

Celebrating Growth Milestones

Cheers to growth and milestones! Celebrating each other's achievements and personal growth moments is like sprinkling magic fairy dust on your love. Mark these occasions with joy and pride, whether it's a small heartfelt gesture or a grand celebration. These moments become cherished memories that symbolize the strength of your love and the journey you've shared together.

As you celebrate growth milestones, take the time to reflect on your journey as a couple. Look back on how far you've come and envision the future you want to create together. Express gratitude for the love, support, and growth you've experienced as a united front. By celebrating these beautiful moments, you reaffirm your commitment to each other and honor the unique love story that continues to unfold.

Embracing Change and Evolution

Change is the rhythm of life, and as a couple growing together, embrace it with open arms. Personal growth may lead to shifts and evolutions within the relationship. Be receptive to these changes, and communicate openly about how they impact your lives. Embrace change as a testament to your dynamic and resilient love story, adapting and growing together through life's beautiful twists and turns.

Embracing change and evolution also means being supportive and understanding during periods of growth. As each of you explores new facets of your identity, show unwavering love and acceptance. Be open to new possibilities and opportunities that arise from personal growth. Remember, love warriors, it is through change and evolution that your love story becomes even more vibrant and alive.

Share one example of how you've navigated a change or evolution within your relationship:

_____

_____

_____

_____

How has that change strengthened your bond as a couple?

_____

_____

_____

_____

Building a Stronger Future Together

Picture the life of your dreams together, because that's exactly what you're capable of building. Align your individual goals with shared aspirations for the future, and envision the legacy you want to leave as a couple. Together, with collaboration, support, and honest communication, you'll create a future that's not just fulfilling but harmonious too. You've got the power to shape your love story, inspiring and uplifting others along the way.

Building a stronger future means making plans and setting goals that encompass your shared dreams. Think of it as a roadmap to your dreams, taking steps together to make them a reality. Remember to cheer each other on and celebrate every milestone you achieve. Your love thrives on personal growth and mutual support, making your journey as a couple all the more extraordinary.

As you both grow and support one another, your love becomes a beacon of hope for future generations of LGBTQ+ couples. Every step you take strengthens your emotional connection, embracing both your individuality and the love you share. Your journey is a celebration of love, compassion, and inclusivity, inspiring all those yet to walk their own rainbow paths. So, embrace your roles as love warriors, lighting up the world with the power of your love and touching lives along the way. Together, you're making a difference, and your love story is proof that love knows no boundaries.

Notes & takeaways from this chapter:

_____

_____

_____

_____

_____

_____

_____

_____

_____

_____

_____

Chapter 7:
Cultivating Gratitude and Building a Lasting Legacy

Embracing the Power of Gratitude

In this section, we're diving into the incredible world of gratitude and its profound impact on your marriage. As a gay couple, expressing gratitude might take on a unique significance, given the world's diverse attitudes toward LGBTQ+ relationships. Amidst the challenges you may face, fostering gratitude in your marriage is a game-changer! Let's explore practical ways to infuse your daily lives with appreciation and acknowledgment.

Gratitude goes beyond a simple "thank you." It's about acknowledging and cherishing the little things that your partner does for you, the love they shower upon you, and the unwavering support they provide. A heartfelt "thank you" for the small gestures can go a long way in creating an emotional connection that strengthens your bond. Moreover, openly expressing gratitude for your partner's love and support can enrich your relationship, reinforcing your love story's unique beauty and the love you share.

By embracing the power of gratitude, you not only cultivate a deeper emotional connection but also build a lasting legacy of love that shines through every aspect of your relationship. Let's make expressing gratitude a regular part of your daily interactions, and witness how this simple yet potent practice transforms your marriage into an oasis of love, trust, and appreciation.

How do you both express gratitude in your marriage, and what are some small gestures you appreciate from each other?

_____

_____

_____

In what ways does openly acknowledging and cherishing each other's love and support strengthen your emotional connection as a couple?

_____

_____

_____

_____

Creating a Legacy of Love and Compassion

As a gay couple, your journey is uniquely inspiring. Reflect on the legacy you wish to build together and how your love story can inspire and uplift other couples.

Your experiences, your triumphs, and even the challenges you've overcome can serve as powerful beacons of hope for others on their own rainbow journeys. Break barriers, challenge stereotypes, and be open about your love. Embrace your role as role models and advocates for the LGBTQ+ community, supporting one another with unwavering dedication.

By sharing your love and experiences, you become agents of change, fostering inclusivity and understanding. Let's find ways to give back and make a positive impact, leaving a legacy of love that echoes through generations to come. Each step you take together on this journey of love becomes a brushstroke in the beautiful canvas of your shared legacy.

Nurturing Inclusivity in Your Marriage

Celebrate the vibrant spirit of inclusivity in your gay marriage, love warriors! Embrace your authentic selves, and let the world witness the magic that unfolds when two extraordinary individuals come together as an exceptional couple.

Advocate for LGBTQ+ rights and representation, both within the safe cocoon of your relationship and beyond. By fostering inclusivity, you not only strengthen your bond as a couple but also cultivate a powerful legacy of love, understanding, and acceptance. Let's embark on open and heartfelt dialogues about diversity, celebrating the beautiful tapestry of the LGBTQ+ community, and embracing the strength that comes from cherishing each other's uniqueness.

Creating an inclusive environment starts with acknowledging and cherishing each other's individuality. Share in each other's experiences, and lend a listening ear to each other's stories. By truly embracing inclusivity, you create a safe haven where both partners feel deeply valued and supported.

Through wholeheartedly embracing inclusivity, you reinforce the unshakable foundation of your love and create a legacy that not only embraces diversity but also becomes a beacon of hope for the world. Let's continue to be the change we wish to see, love warriors, and together, we'll leave a lasting legacy of love and acceptance for generations to come. Embrace the power of inclusivity and let it infuse your marriage with an unmatched sense of unity and strength.

How can you foster inclusivity in your marriage and create a safe and welcoming space where both you and your partner feel celebrated for your authentic selves?

_____

_____

_____

_____

_____

Fostering Resilience and Overcoming Challenges

Love warriors, get ready for an empowering journey of resilience! According to a study by the Williams Institute at UCLA School of Law, LGBTQ+ couples may encounter external pressures and prejudices in their journey. But fear not! In this section, we'll explore how you can conquer any obstacle that comes your way, united as an unstoppable force.

Embrace challenges as stepping stones for growth and personal development. Research published in the Journal of Marriage and Family shows that couples who tackle adversities together not only fortify their bond but also deepen their emotional connection. By facing adversity side by side, you create a lasting legacy of strength and determination, serving as an inspiration for others to stand strong amidst life's storms.

Let's take a moment to celebrate the triumphs of your love story. Studies have revealed that LGBTQ+ couples, despite unique challenges, often experience a growth in love and commitment. Your journey as a couple is a testament to resilience and the unyielding power of love. You've proven that love knows no bounds, and your unwavering commitment shines as a beacon of hope for others.

As you stand united, your love becomes a legacy of strength, an inspiration to love fearlessly and fiercely. Together, you are rewriting the narrative of LGBTQ+ love, showing the world that love conquers all. So, love warriors, keep your spirits high, and remember, you've got the power to conquer anything that comes your way! Let your love shine as a testament to the beauty and resilience of gay marriages.

Extending Your Legacy

The topic of your legacy can't be complete without discussing and diving into the conversations about your viewpoints and aspirations for extending it. It's all about making those big decisions together, whether you have dreams of growing your family or finding contentment without kiddos.

So, picture this: you and your partner, sitting down with a cup of coffee (or a cocktail if that's more your style), having a real, intimate talk about your future together. You know, that dream of building a family? Adoption, fostering, or whatever floats your boat – it's all on the table! And guess what? Over 60% of LGBTQ+ couples consider adoption or fostering as a way to grow their family. It's amazing how we're shaping a legacy of love, compassion, and inclusivity.

But hey, hold up! Not everyone feels the parenting vibes, and that's completely cool too! You can totally find contentment without kids, focusing on your passions, careers, and making a difference in your community. You'll be proud to know that your impact can be just as profound without little ones running around. It's your journey, your choices, and your legacy – no cookie-cutter mold needed!

The best part is that as gay married couples, we're redefining what legacy means, smashing stereotypes, and creating our own path. We're like trailblazers, carving out a legacy that's as unique as each and every one of us. There's no one-size-fits-all, and that's what makes it fun and exciting!

So, let's get down to it – those intimate conversations that strengthen your bond and help you navigate your future together. These chats aren't about getting all philosophical or quoting ancient philosophers; it's about connecting on a deep level, understanding each other's dreams, fears, and aspirations. It's like a tag-team adventure – you're in it together, supporting and cheering each other on!

Whether you're a family-builder or living your best child-free life, the key is to have these conversations with love, respect, and a dash of humor. Embrace the uniqueness of your journey as a gay couple, and let your legacy be a reflection of your love, joy, and the positive impact you bring to the world.

How do you both feel about the idea of building a family together?

_____

_____

_____

What is your top priority when it comes to creating a loving and supportive family environment?

_____

_____

Have you discussed the potential challenges and rewards of parenthood as a gay couple? Elaborate on a few below:

_____

What kind of support systems do you have in place to help you navigate the journey of parenthood if you choose that route?

_____

_____

_____

How do you envision your future family dynamic (kid(s)s or not), and how can you work together to make that vision a reality?

_____

_____

_____

_____

_____

_____

_____

_____

_____

Notes & takeaways from this chapter:

_____

_____

_____

_____

_____

_____

_____

_____

_____

_____

_____

_____

_____

_____

_____

_____

_____

Conclusion:
The Rainbow You've Manifested

Congratulations, love warriors, on completing The Rainbow Journey! It's been one empowering adventure, and I'm so proud of the incredible growth and connection you've cultivated along the way. In the beginning, we celebrated the uniqueness of your love story, honoring your individuality as a powerhouse gay couple. You embraced your extraordinary selves, and that's what makes your love shine so brightly! From the very start, you both recognized that your journey as a couple is something special, and you've continued to nurture that spark throughout this incredible journey.

Then we dove deep into the art of communication, the heart and soul of any rock-solid marriage. We tailored some awesome techniques just for you, helping you deepen that emotional connection and handle anything life throws your way. Through open and honest conversations, you've strengthened your bond, allowing your love to flourish even amidst the challenges that may come your way. As a result, you've built a strong foundation for a lasting and fulfilling relationship. Navigating family and social dynamics might've been a rollercoaster, but you did it like the champs you are! You found insights and strategies to build positive relationships with your supportive peeps and gracefully handle the challenging ones. As a gay couple, you've faced unique obstacles and biases, but you've demonstrated resilience and unity, showing the world the beauty of love and inclusivity.

And oh boy, collaborative decision-making and conflict resolution – that's some serious ninja-level stuff! By tackling obstacles together, you built a safe space for personal growth and love to thrive. You two are unstoppable! Your ability to work as a team, supporting each other's dreams and aspirations, has paved the way for a future full of endless possibilities. We then explored the magic of cultivating intimacy and affection, discovering how small gestures can make a world of difference in your relationship. From nurturing emotional connections to date night ideas, you've learned the secrets to keeping that spark alive and burning bright. Your love has become a flame that warms the hearts of those around you, leaving a lasting impression on all who have the privilege to witness it.

Finally, we unleashed the power of personal growth within your marriage. Supporting each other's journeys while growing together – that's what it's all about! Your love is like a delicious cake, and personal growth is the icing on top. By encouraging each other to flourish individually, you've created a dynamic partnership that continues to evolve and flourish. And let's not forget about the cherry on that cake – gratitude! By showing appreciation for each other's awesomeness, you've created a lasting legacy of love, compassion, and inclusivity. Your love is a shining beacon, guiding others on their own rainbow journeys. Your story serves as an inspiration for many, a testament to the transformative power of love and the beauty of forging your own path as a gay couple.

So, as you stand at the end of The Rainbow Journey, remember that the adventure doesn't stop here. Keep nurturing your love, keep growing together, and keep inspiring others with your extraordinary bond. Your legacy is a testament to the power of love. Your love story is unique, inspiring, and oh-so-powerful. You're writing a narrative of resilience and commitment that will echo through time and touch the lives of others. Keep shining, love warriors, and know that your love is changing the world, one rainbow at a time. Cheers to the journey ahead, and to a lifetime of love, laughter, happiness and success, together.

Reflection:
Questions & Activities to Continue the Journey

What are some simple ways we can express love and affection for each other every day?

_____

_____

_____

How can we create a safe and open space for honest communication in our marriage?

_____

_____

_____

What are our favorite activities to do together that bring us joy and strengthen our bond?

_____

_____

_____

How can we support each other's individual growth and personal goals?

_____

_____

What are some small gestures or surprises we can do for each other to keep the romance alive?

_____

_____

_____

How do we handle disagreements or conflicts in a loving and understanding manner?

_____

_____

_____

What are some shared values or beliefs that we can build our marriage upon?

_____

_____

_____

How can we prioritize quality time together amidst busy schedules?

_____

_____

What are some ways we can show appreciation and gratitude for each other on a consistent basis?

_____

_____

_____

How can we maintain a healthy work-life balance to nurture our relationship?

_____

_____

_____

What are our favorite memories together, and how can we create more of those moments?

_____

_____

_____

_____

_____

_____

How can we cultivate trust and vulnerability in our relationship?

_____

_____

_____

How can we show support and understanding for each other's emotions and feelings?

_____

_____

_____

What are some fun and creative ways we can surprise each other with small gifts or acts of kindness?

_____

_____

_____

How can we keep the spark alive in our marriage through playful and flirtatious interactions?

_____

_____

What are our individual love languages, and how can we meet each other's needs?

_____

_____

_____

How can we continue to grow and evolve as a couple while embracing our unique journey?

_____

_____

_____

What are some shared goals or dreams we want to accomplish together in the future?

_____

_____

_____

How can we cultivate trust and vulnerability in our relationship?

_____

_____

What are some ways we can support each other's self-care and well-being? What are some ways we can practice self care together?

_____

_____

_____

_____

_____

What are some of the top takeaways you've learned from "The Rainbow Journey," and how do you plan on implementing them?

_____

_____

_____

_____

_____

_____

_____

_____

Notes & takeaways:

_____

_____

_____

_____

_____

_____

_____

_____

_____

_____

_____

_____

_____

_____

_____

_____

Notes & takeaways:

_____

_____

_____

_____

_____

_____

_____

_____

_____

_____

_____

_____

_____

_____

_____

Notes & takeaways:

_____

_____

_____

_____

_____

_____

_____

_____

_____

_____

_____

_____

_____

_____

_____

_____

Notes & takeaways:

_____

_____

_____

_____

_____

_____

_____

_____

_____

_____

_____

_____

_____

_____

_____

_____

_____

_____

Hi! I'm Sky.

I'm a 33-year-old husband turned writer, designer, travel enthusiast, and lover of all things creative. I'm here to share real-talk insights into the rollercoaster ride of married life for all you fabulous gay couples out there! When my close friends were about to tie the knot, I wanted to gift them something truly meaningful and practical. But after hours of searching, I couldn't find anything that hit the mark. That's when it dawned on me - why not draw from my own experiences in my gay marriage and those of my peers around me to create "The Rainbow Journey: A Guide to Married Life for Gay Couples." A self-help book capturing the essence of what my friends were about to embark on - a journey of love and commitment as a married gay couple, with tips on navigating this adventure.

From tackling everyday challenges to handling unique obstacles faced by LGBTQ+ couples. As a fellow traveler in the realm of gay marriage, I share practical tips, fun anecdotes as well as personal struggles and triumphs my husband and I encountered in our own marriage, shedding light on how to navigate this exciting voyage of commitment together.

With this book, you demonstrate that your journey as a gay couple is not only valid but also capable of making a meaningful impact on others. Your colorful love story is a beacon of light for those navigating similar paths, showing that love knows no boundaries and can triumph over any challenge. By embracing this gay marriage roadmap, you celebrate your unique love and inspire others to do the same with pride. Thank you for reading, and congratulations on your marriage. May your Rainbow Journey shine brightly, leaving a trail of love and inspiration for others to follow, now and into eternity.

With Love, Sky

Made in United States
Orlando, FL
14 December 2024

55574665R00046